101 Great Value Wines
for under €10

GW00729203

101

GREAT WINES
FOR UNDER €10

JOHN WILSON

A & A FARMAR

British Library Cataloguing in Publication Data
A CIP catalogue record for this book is available from the British Library

ISBN 1-899047-35-2

Published by
A. & A. Farmar
78 Ranelagh Village, Dublin 6
Ireland
Tel (01) 496 3625 Fax (01) 497 0107
afarmar@iol.ie
www.aafarmar.ie

Cover design by Brosna Press
Typesetting by Bookworks
Printed and bound by GraphyCems

CONTENTS

INTRODUCTION

When I first started out on this book, I thought it might be hard to come up with 101 genuinely drinkable wines for under €10. In fact, the problem has been the opposite—in addition to the great value, inexpensive wines described here, I have a list of fifty more wines that I found very difficult to leave out. Yet just a few short years ago, you had to pay €12 or more to find a decent bottle of wine.

The wine business in Ireland has never been so competitive. Look along the shelves of any supermarket or off-licence and you will see a huge array of wines on offer at less than €10. Many of these are very good indeed, and offer the intelligent buyer very pleasurable drinking.

These days, there is simply no excuse for poor or undrinkable wine. A word of warning, however: there are limits to the winemaker's ingenuity—it is very difficult to make drinkable wine at €5.99 or less. Most of the wines in this book cost between €8 and €10. With one or two exceptions, this is where quality wine starts. Even at €10, there is no shortage of thin, weedy wines that won't put a smile on anyone's face.

This book aims to take the guesswork out of buying a bottle of wine. Over the last year, I have tasted thousands of wines. I have selected the very best under €10 and in every different style. There will be many familiar names, and quite a few you may not have come across before. They have one thing in common: they offer better value for money than their counterparts.

Some of the wines are available from a huge number of off-licences, supermarkets and wine shops all over the country, too many to be listed individually. In these instances, I have listed 15–20 off-licences spread across the country, and indicated that the wine is available in other outlets too. Other wines are slightly less widely available but I do hope that no matter where you live, you will find it easy to buy a good proportion of them.

Prices for particular wines can vary from shop to shop. In most cases, I have quoted the recommended retail price given to me by the importer. Retailers are free to charge what they like (and remember smaller shops may have to pay higher prices to the suppliers than supermarkets which buy in bulk), so you may find some wines cost more in some outlets than €10.

There are few greater pleasures in life than sitting around a table with family or friends eating a simple meal, and drinking a few glasses of decent wine. The choice in this book is a personal one, and reflects my own tastes. Wine offers a fantastic range of exciting flavours. I hope this book will encourage you to try out new wines, and make some interesting discoveries—all without breaking the bank.

Happy drinking!
John Wilson

FOOD AND WINE

Having worked in wine shops for many years, I know that people are often terrified of serving the 'wrong' wine with a particular food. It is true that some wines and foods are a match made in heaven, but please, please remember that most wine goes with most food. Most food tastes far better with wine, too. Keep a few basic principles in mind, and you won't go wrong. There are no rules, only what you enjoy yourself. Do not allow yourself to be bullied. Below are a few guidelines to help you get more from your glass of wine.

Guidelines for matching food and wine

In general, try to match full-bodied wines with powerful food, lighter wines with lighter dishes.

Fish tends to be fairly bland, and needs something to liven it up. That's why it is served with vinegar in your local chipper, or with a slice of lemon, tartare sauce, or a white wine sauce in fancy establishments. White wine has much higher acidity than red wine. The sharpness livens up the fish; at the same time, the fish makes the wine seem smoother. Therefore it makes sense to serve white wine with most fish, although some light, fresh red wines go very nicely with full-flavoured fish such as salmon or tuna.

Meat Red wine goes better with meat. Why? All red wine contains varying amounts of tannin, acids which makes your mouth dry and your teeth feel furry. The fat in meat, and the blood in rare steaks smoothes these tannins out. At the same time, the tannins provide a 'cut', and make the meat taste far better. But don't feel you must stick to reds. If you prefer white wine, full-bodied whites are great with chicken, pork, and even lamb or beef.

Cheese Most people serve red wine with cheese. It is true that hard, cheddar-type cheese tends to go best with red wines; but blue cheese goes very well with sweet wine or port; and the rest tend to taste better with white wines, particularly goat's cheese, which is a perfect match for Sauvignon.

Vegetarian dishes The same principles apply to vegetarian as to any other food—match lighter dishes with lighter wines, saving the powerful wines for more robust fare. Light whites go well with salads, dips, and leek, onion or courgette tarts. Try fruity whites and reds with creamy or tomato-based pasta dishes, cous-cous, and risotto. Vegetable bakes, mushrooms and grilled or barbecued vegetables need powerful wines, full of flavour.

Things to watch out for

Very hot or spicy foods can kill a delicate wine. I find big Australian Shiraz goes best with hot curries. Aromatic wines from the New World, such as Sauvignon, Pinot Gris and Gewurztraminer also go well with spicy, herby Thai dishes.

Acidic sauces such as tomato sauce tend to go better with wines that have a similar acidity.

Vinegar is wine that has gone off; it tends to make any wine taste thin and mean. Use sparingly, or try lemon juice (or even white wine) instead.

Sweet fruits with meat such as cranberry sauce can make a dry wine seem very acidic, as can either sweet and sour sauces, or chutney which are both sweet and vinegary at the same time.

Versatile wines

If you are unsure what wine to pick, or you are serving a variety of foods, the following are good all-rounders—multi-purpose wines that will happily partner pretty well anything you can throw at them.

White wines Light and refreshing wines such as Pinot Grigio, Sauvignon or Riesling, or the rounder and fruitier Semillon and unoaked Chardonnay are all a safe bet, wines that go well with everything from salads, vegetable dishes, fish, seafood, spicy dishes to pasta and even pizza. Provided they are not too high in alcohol, you can also serve them at drinks parties or before a meal.

Red wines Lighter and fruitier wines such as Merlot, Pinot Noir, and Tempranillo, or the more powerful and full-bodied Côtes du Rhône and Aussie Shiraz are all very versatile wines because of their lighter tannins. They enhance just about any food, including roasts, casseroles, cold meats, pizzas, pasta, hard cheeses, and vegetable stews with beans.

BUYING, STORING AND SERVING WINE

Some people find wine shops intimidating. Most are actually friendly places, staffed by knowledgeable people only too willing to help. Don't be afraid to ask questions or ask for advice.

No decent wine merchant will try to sell you a dodgy bottle, or something you don't like. They want you to come back—this week, next week, and every week for years to come. After all, that is the way they make money!

If you are buying wine in bulk, a case or more, you should expect a discount of 5–10 per cent: why not ask for 10? Some shops will offer a free bottle of something else. Most will be happy to supply glasses, ice and anything else you might need for your party.

Faulty wine

Very occasionally, you will come across a faulty wine. Any proper supermarket or shop will be happy to replace it, or refund your money without quibble. Remember the Sale of Goods Act applies to wine as well. A badly-made, or incorrectly stored wine can smell of vinegar, nail-polish remover, sherry, or rotten eggs. Corked wines are tainted with a nasty, musty smell and taste by a faulty cork. The aroma reminds me of dirty dishcloths. Wines with screwcaps or plastic corks do not suffer from this problem. The basic rule concerning faulty wines is: if it doesn't smell right, bring it back!

Storing wine

Wine is a fairly robust liquid, and can take a certain amount of punishment without any real damage being done. Most of us drink our wine within days of buying it. In that case, it doesn't really matter where you keep it, provided you avoid extreme heat.

Most white wines (although not all) at under €10 should be drunk within a year to eighteen months of the vintage. Red wine tends to last better, and can often improve with keeping. However, the vast majority of red wines should be drunk within two to three years of the vintage.

If you want to store your wine for months or even years, it gets a little complicated. Few modern houses have a cellar in which to store wine, but this need not deter you from laying down a few bottles that will improve with time.

Try to keep your wine in a cool, dark environment, free from sudden changes in temperature. A cupboard under the stairs, a garage, or a cool room will do. Just avoid garages that get very hot in the summer, and don't put the wine next to a radiator or boiler. A temperature of 10–15°C is perfect, but a few degrees more won't cause any harm.

Strong light can also harm wine, so keep it in a dark place. If your wine has a natural cork, it should be kept lying down. If it has a screw-cap or plastic cork, standing up is fine.

Serving wine

White wine should be served chilled, at about 8–10°C, a little warmer than most fridges. It is better not to put it in an ice bucket—very cold wine tastes of nothing. I keep a *Rapid Ice*, a sort of lagging jacket, in the freezer at all times, which will chill a bottle in about ten minutes.

Red wines are best at around 15–18°C degrees, room temperature back in Victorian times. These days most houses are warmer, so heating a bottle is rarely necessary. Remember the wine will warm up gradually once you pour it. If you do need to apply some heat, don't stick your bottle in front of a fire. Instead, immerse it in lukewarm water (i.e. blood temperature) for about five minutes. A red wine that is too warm will taste soupy and alcoholic; too cold and it will seem very tannic.

A friend of mine has a great way of preparing a bottle for drinking quickly. Fill your decanter or jug with hot water for five minutes. Pour it out, and immediately pour in your cold, tannic red wine. The combination of air and the warm glass will work wonders on the wine in just five minutes.

Corkscrews

There is a huge variety of corkscrews available. Check that your corkscrew has a worm-like spiral, and not a solid screw—these tend to rip the cork, rather than pulling it out.

Glasses

Serving wine in decent glasses makes an amazing difference. Large tulip shaped glasses are ideal for concentrating the aromas of the wine. Plain glass reveals the colour of the wine better than cut glass. By filling the glass a third to a half full you will be

able to swirl the wine around, and allow the aromas
to develop.

Decanters

Decanters can look great, and add a real touch of class
to a dinner party. They are only absolutely necessary
if your wine has a lot of sediment, or if it needs
aeration. Decanting can benefit many young red
wines, but it is not essential.

WINE WORDS

Wine is one of the most complex drinks, with an amazing array of wonderful flavours, yet nothing arouses so much ridicule than the seemingly pretentious words wine people use to describe a wine. Everything is invoked from plums, strawberries, pineapples and other fruits to flowers, leather, tar, and even kerosene. How, you might ask, can a wine taste of kerosene, and if it did, would you want to drink it?

The problem is this: we have very few words in the English language to describe flavours. What does cheese taste of, or beef? We can say they have lots of flavour, or they are mild. We can describe them as sweet, salty, sour, or bitter, but this still doesn't describe the full range of flavours. So we have to compare a wine's flavours to fruit, spice, wood, herbs and the like to try to give an idea of its taste.

I am not a fan of long-winded, complicated descriptions. In this book, I have tried to keep them as short as possible, while still giving an accurate picture of how the wines taste.

The Wines

LIGHT AND REFRESHING WHITE

Light and refreshing white wines are zippy and fresh with plenty of lively acidity. They generally have lighter fruit and lower alcohol than the round and fruity whites in the next section. They are ideal by themselves, or with fish, seafood and less powerful dishes.

ALAIN BRUMONT GROS MANSENG/SAUVIGNON BLANC VIN DE PAYS DES CÔTES DE GASCOGNE 2004

South West France

€9.99

Grape: Gros Manseng, Sauvignon Blanc
Alcohol: 13%

Plenty of aromas—gooseberries and grapefruit, and a vibrant fresh palate of crisp green fruits.
Great on its own, or with lighter fish dishes; it would also go very nicely with goats' cheese dishes.

Stockists: Dublin – Liston's, Camden St; The Celtic Whiskey Shop, Dawson St. **Kilkenny** – Le Caveau, Kilkenny.
Roscommon – Aherne's, Boyle. **Waterford** – La Boulangerie, Waterford. **Wexford** – Pettit's Supermarkets

ANTINORI CAMPOGRANDE ORVIETO CLASSICO 2003
Umbria, Italy
€9.99

Grape: Procanico, Grechetto, Verdelho, Drupeggio & Malvasia
Alcohol: 12%

Light, with very soft, ripe fruit, finishing dry with a lovely touch of bitter almonds on the finish.
Drink this as an aperitif, or with seafood or fish, particularly in pastas and salads.

Stockists: Almost nationwide – Eurospar; SPAR; SuperValu; Superquinn. **Dublin** – Cellars Wine Warehouse, Naas Rd; Gables, Foxrock; Martha's Vineyard, Rathfarnham; McCabe's, Blackrock & Foxrock; McHugh's, Kilbarrack & Artane; No. One Vintage, Goatstown; Nolan's, Clontarf; O'Briens Wine Off-licences; Redmond's, Ranelagh; Savage's, Swords; Sweeney's, Glasnevin

CHÂTEAU HAUT RIAN BORDEAUX
2004

Bordeaux, France

€9.90

Grape: Sauvignon Blanc, Sémillon
Alcohol: 12.5%

Lively but rounded light fresh green fruits and an impressive long, dry finish.
An all-purpose white, great by itself or with most fish and seafood dishes.

Stockists: Westmeath – Wines Direct

CHÂTEAU PIQUE-SÈGUE MONTRAVEL 2003

South West France

€9.99

Grape: Sauvignon Blanc, Sémillon, Muscadelle
Alcohol: 12.5%

One of my favourites, and a wine with a difference. Medium-bodied, with beautifully rounded ripe pears and quince set off by some mineral acidity and a dry finish.
This would go very nicely with robust fish, such as salmon, or with chicken and pork. Try it with a starter of pâtés and cold meats.

Stockists: Dublin – Cheers at the Foxhunter, Lucan; Corks, Terenure; Jus de Vine, Portmarnock; McHugh's, Kilbarrack & Artane; Molloy's Liquor Stores; Morton's, Ranelagh; O'Neill's, South Circular Rd; Rowan's, Rathfarnham. **Kildare** – Fullam's, Rathangan. **Roscommon** – Daly's, Boyle. **Wicklow** – Caprani's, Ashford

CUVÉE ORÉLIE VIN DE PAYS DES COTEAUX DE L'ARDÈCHE 2004

Rhône Valley, France

€8.95

Grape: Chardonnay, Sauvignon Blanc
Alcohol: 12%

Light, elegant apple fruits, with lovely floral aromas, and a crisp dry finish.
Perfect by itself, or with light seafood, fish or chicken dishes. Made from a blend of Chardonnay (used to make all white Burgundy) and Sauvignon Blanc (used to make Sancerre and Pouilly-Fumé).

Stockists: Dublin – Donnybrook Fair; Michael's Wines, Mount Merrion; Mitchell & Son, Kildare St & Glasthule; On the Grapevine, Dalkey & Booterstown; Red Island Wines, Skerries; The Grape Escape, Lucan. **Galway** – Harvest, Galway & Oranmore; Probus Wines, Oughterard; The Wine Cluster, Moycullen. **Wexford** – Pettit's Supermarkets. **Wicklow** – Wicklow Wine Co., Wicklow

DE WETSHOF DANIE DE WET CHARDONNAY SUR LIE 2004

Robertson, South Africa

€9.95

Grape: Chardonnay
Alcohol: 14%

Light, with a slight yeasty touch, and lovely crisp, zesty apple fruit. A real bargain from one of the best makers of white wine in South Africa.

A great all-rounder. Perfect party wine, or to sip with friends. Otherwise with light fish, seafood, and even chicken dishes. Another of the best-value wines on the market.

Stockists: Carlow – Next Door, Carlow. **Cork** – Next Door, Cork & Glanmire. **Dublin** – Cheers, Shankill; Deveney's, South Circular Rd & Dundrum; Gibney's, Malahide; Londis, Morehampton Rd; Shiels' Londis, Malahide; SuperValu, Killester; SuperValu, Malahide; The Celtic Whiskey Shop, Dawson St; The Vintry, Rathgar. **Limerick** – Next Door, Patrickswell. **Mayo** – Next Door, Belmullet. **Meath** – Next Door, Enfield. **Wexford** – Centra, Wexford. **Westmeath** – Next Door, Athlone. **Wexford** – Pettit's Supermarkets. **Wexford** – SuperValu, Tramore

DELHEIM THREE SPRINGS WHITE 2004

Stellenbosch, South Africa

€7.69

Grape: Sauvignon Blanc, Chenin Blanc
Alcohol: 13.5%

Amazing value—a delicious wine with fresh, light grapefruit and melons, and a soft finish.
A perfect, easy-drinking, all-purpose wine that would go down a bomb at a party.

Stockists: Dublin – O'Briens Wine Off-licences

DOMAINE DE SAINT-LANNES VIN DE PAYS DES CÔTES DE GASCOGNE 2004

South West France

€8.99

Grape: Colombard, Gros Manseng, Ugni Blanc
Alcohol: 12%

Zingy, fresh, crisp green fruits shot through with lemon zest. Light and very tasty.
Drink this on its own if you like fresh, crisp wines, otherwise it would be great with mussels and other seafood.

Stockists: Dublin – O'Briens Wine Off-licences

DOMAINE D'ESPÉRANCE
CUVEÉ D'OR
VIN DE PAYS DES LANDES 2004
South West France
€9.50

Grape: Gros Manseng, Sauvignon Blanc, Colombard
Alcohol: 12%

A wine I love—crisp, firm, steely dry wine, with mouth-watering cool apple fruits.
Great by itself or just made to go with seafood and lighter fish dishes. Perfect with a bowl of mussels.

Stockists: Donegal – Dicey Reilly's, Ballyshannon.
Dublin – Anderson's, Glasnevin; Douglas Food Co., Donnybrook; Mitchell & Son, Kildare St & Glasthule. **Kerry** – French Flair, Tralee; O'Driscoll's, Caherciveen. **Roscommon** – Heran's, Boyle

DR LOOSEN RIESLING 2003
Mosel-Saar-Ruwer, Germany
€9.99

Grape: Riesling
Alcohol: 9.5%

Charming light floral aromas and elegant apple fruits, finishing off-dry.
One to sip in the shade after a hard day's work in the garden or if you are lazy, just lolling in the grass.

Stockists: Almost nationwide – Superquinn. **Dublin** – Cellars Wine Warehouse, Naas Rd; Coolers, Swords; Donnybrook Fair; Gibney's, Malahide; Higgins, Clonskeagh; McHugh's, Kilbarrack & Artane; Nolan's, Clontarf; O'Briens Wine Off-licences; Redmond's, Ranelagh; SPAR, Rathcoole; The Lifeboat, Skerries. **Louth** – McPhail's, Drogheda. **Mayo** – Gaffney's, Ballina & Castlebar. **Meath** – Killian's, Trim. **Waterford** – Waterford World of Wine

DRAYTON'S OAKEY CREEK SEMILLON/CHARDONNAY 2004
South East Australia
€9.70

Grape: Semillon, Chardonnay
Alcohol: 12%

This is great-value wine—very high-quality, light, delicate grape and ripe melon fruits, with a delicious zesty touch.
Light fruit and low alcohol make this ideal as a party wine, as a summer aperitif, or for just sitting around with friends.

Stockists: Westmeath – Wines Direct

FLAGSTONE NOON GUN WHITE 2004
Coastal Region, South Africa
€7.99

Grape: Sauvignon Blanc, Riesling, Chardonnay, Chenin Blanc
Alcohol: 12.5%

Fresh and zesty, with lovely rounded pear and mango fruits. Great name, great wine.
Try it by itself or with most Asian fish and chicken dishes.

Stockists: Dublin – Oddbins

FONTANA CANDIDA FRASCATI
2004
Latium, Italy
€8.99

Grape: Trebbiano, Malvasia di Candida, Malvasia del Lazio
Alcohol: 12%

Very light and crisp, with lively grapefruits and apples, finishing dry.
Try it with any seafood dish—it would be perfect with crab, prawns or scallops.

Stockists: Almost nationwide – Centra; SuperValu; Superquinn. **Dublin** – O'Briens Wine Off-licences.
Wexford – Pettit's Supermarkets

HONORÉ DE BERTICOT SAUVIGNON CÔTES DE DURAS 2004

South West France

€9.99

Grape: Sauvignon Blanc
Alcohol: 13%

One of those wines nearly everybody likes. Relatively big and fresh, with plenty of citrus flavours to match the green fruits.
Multi-purpose wine that will partner bigger fish dishes, as well as chicken and pork, very nicely indeed.

Stockists: Almost nationwide – Next Door. **Dublin** – Gibney's, Malahide; On the Grapevine, Dalkey & Booterstown; Searson's, Monkstown; The Grape Escape, Lucan. **Tipperary** – Country Choice, Nenagh. **Wicklow** – Avoca Handweavers, Wicklow; Murtagh's, Enniskerry

INYCON FIANO
IGT SICILIA 2004
Sicily, Italy
€7.99

Grape: Fiano
Alcohol: 13.5%

A lovely dry wine, filled with apple and pineapple fruit, shot through with just enough refreshing acidity, and a dry finish. Fiano, a very old grape variety from Campania in southern Italy, was grown by the ancient Romans.

A great all-purpose wine, suitable for parties, drinking on its own, or with fish, seafood or chicken dishes.

Stockists: Almost nationwide – Dunnes Stores

J P BRANCO
VR TERRAS DO SADO NV
Setúbal, Portugal
€6.99

Grape: Moscatel, Fernão Pires
Alcohol: 11%

Lightly aromatic, with very light, crisp grapefruit and
grapes, finishing off-dry.
The perfect party wine, particularly during summer.

Stockists: Almost nationwide – Centra; SuperValu; Superquinn

LAURENT MIQUEL CHARDONNAY-VIOGNIER VIN DE PAYS D'OC 2004

Languedoc, France

€7.99

Grape: Chardonnay, Viognier
Alcohol: 13%

A light to medium-bodied wine brimful of nectarines, pears and apples, wrapped in a lively core of lemony freshness.
Most chicken and lighter pork dishes, but light and fruity enough to drink on its own.

Stockists: Almost nationwide – Dunnes Stores

MARQUÉS DE CÁCERES RIOJA 2003
North Spain
€8.99

Grape: Viura
Alcohol: 12%

A very attractive, light, easy-to-drink wine, aromatic, with fresh, zingy, crisp apple and green fruits. Great by itself, before a meal, or for a girls' night in; good with lighter fish and white meats. One of the very best inexpensive Spanish white wines.

Stockists: Cork – Bradley's; **Dublin** – Bennett's, Howth Carvill's, Camden St; Donnybrook Fair; Eurospar, Rathcoole; Jus de Vine, Portmarnock; Kelly's Wine Vault, Artane; Quinn's, Drumcondra; Redmond's, Ranelagh; Sweeney's, Glasnevin; The Lord Mayor's, Swords. **Galway** – Harvest, Galway & Oranmore; Joyce's, Galway & Headford; The Vineyard, Galway. **Louth** – Callan's, Dundalk; Egan's, Drogheda. **Limerick** – Next Door, Raheen. **Sligo** – Foley's, Sligo. **Wicklow** – Halpin's Fine Wines, Wicklow & Gorey. **Westmeath** – Next Door, Athlone. **Wexford** – Pettit's Supermarkets

MARQUÉS DE RISCAL RUEDA 2004
North Spain
€9.99

Grape: Verdejo, Viura
Alcohol: 12.5%

Delicious, fresh and full of ripe green fruits (apples, greengages and pears), finishing dry.
A great all-rounder—perfect on its own before dinner, with friends, or with a variety of lighter foods—salads come to mind. It would also make a great party wine.

Stockists: Almost nationwide – Centra; Londis; SuperValu.
Dublin – Bin No. 9, Goatstown; Cheers at Baker's Corner; Cheers at The Arc, Liffey Valley Shopping Centre; Cheers, Ballinteer; Cheers, Lucan; Cheers, Shankill; Cheers, Walkinstown; Cheers, Whitehall; Deveney's, South Circular Rd & Dundrum;
(continued on next page)

Higgins, Clonskeagh; McCabe's, Blackrock & Foxrock; McHugh's, Kilbarrack & Artane; Molloy's Liquor Stores; Morton's, Ranelagh; Nolan's, Clontarf; O'Briens Wine Off-licences; On the Grapevine, Dalkey & Booterstown; Savage's, Swords; Silver Granite, Palmerstown; The Vintry, Rathgar. **Wicklow** – Cheers at The Wicklow Arms, Delgany

MONTES SAUVIGNON BLANC 2004
Curicó Valley, Chile
€8.99

Grape: Sauvignon Blanc
Alcohol: 12.5%

Broad, ripe gooseberry and grapefruit fruits in a fairly rich style of Sauvignon.
A good all-purpose wine to go with lighter foods—salads, quiches, goats' cheese or fish dishes.

Stockists: Almost nationwide – Dunnes Stores; Eurospar; Londis; Next Door; SuperValu; Superquinn; Tesco. **Cork** – Blarney Off-licence. **Dublin** – Coolers, Applewood; Gerry's, Skerries; Redmond's, Ranelagh. **Galway** – Joyce's, Galway & Headford. **Limerick** – Fine Wines, Limerick. Ivan's, Caherdavin. **Tipperary** – Eldon's, Clonmel. **Waterford** – Ardkeen Stores, Waterford

PETER LEHMANN
BAROSSA RIESLING 2004
Barossa Valley, Australia
€9.99

Grape: Riesling
Alcohol: 12%

Consistently one of the best-value wines you can buy.
Fresh pineapple and green-apple fruits in a delicious,
light dry white.
An all-purpose wine that you could happily sip on its
own, or serve with fish or seafood.

Stockists: Almost nationwide – SPARs (selected); Superquinn.
Dublin – Boomers, Clondalkin; Coolers, Swords; Corks, Terenure;
(continued on next page)

Jus de Vine, Portmarnock; Marron's Londis, Tallaght; Morton's, Ranelagh; O'Briens Wine Off-licences; O'Neills, South Circular Rd; Rowan's, Rathfarnham; The Vintry, Rathgar. **Galway** – The Vineyard, Galway. **Louth** – Callan's, Dundalk. **Meath** – Coolers, Clonee. **Mayo** – Gaffney's, Ballina & Castlebar. **Waterford** – Ardkeen Stores, Waterford

PETER LEHMANN BAROSSA SEMILLON 2002

Barossa Valley, Australia

€9.99

Grape: Semillon
Alcohol: 12%

As with the Peter Lehmann Riesling, a great-value wine—lightly fruity, with fresh lime and easy-drinking green fruit.
An ideal summer wine, a party wine, or for sipping whilst chatting with friends.

Stockists: Almost nationwide – Superquinn. **Cork –** O'Donovan's, Cork. **Dublin** – Cellars Wine Warehouse, Naas Rd; *(continued on next page)*

Marron's Londis, Tallaght; O'Neills, South Circular Rd; Redmond's, Ranelagh; The Vintry, Rathgar. **Galway** – The Vineyard, Galway. **Louth** – Callan's, Dundalk; Egan's, Drogheda. **Roscommon** – Daly's, Boyle. **Wexford** – Greenacres, Wexford

PONTE PIETRA
TREBBIANO/GARGANEGA
IGT VENETO 2004

Veneto, Italy

€7.99

Grape: Trebbiano, Garganega
Alcohol: 12%

Great-value wine, light and fresh with just enough crisp apple fruits.
The Italians would drink it with fish and seafood, but it would also make an excellent aperitif.

Stockists: Dublin – Red Island Wines, Skerries.
Wexford – Pettit's Supermarkets

RST ALPHA ZETA SOAVE IGT VENETO 2004

Veneto, Italy

€9.95

Grape: Garganega
Alcohol: 12.5%

Soave as it should be—light, fresh, crisp pear and apple fruits, with a delicious zestiness.
A lovely light aperitif, or the perfect match for plain seafood and fish.

Stockists: Cork – O'Donovan's, Cork. **Dublin** – Donnybrook Fair; McHugh's, Kilbarrack & Artane; Redmond's, Ranelagh. **Meath** – The Drinkstore, Navan

SECANO ESTATE
SAUVIGNON BLANC 2004
Leyda Valley, Chile
€9.99

Grape: Sauvignon Blanc
Alcohol: 13.5%

A very fine light, crisp, racy wine, with light aromatic green fruits, finishing dry.
Delicious lively wine at an excellent price. Perfect summer wine, enjoyed sitting out on the patio, or as an aperitif. It is one of my 'chef's' wines, to be sipped while I make the dinner.

Stockists: Almost nationwide – Marks & Spencer

TESCO'S FINEST
MUSCADET DE SÈVRE ET MAINE
SUR LIE 2003

Loire Valley, France

€8.89

Grape: Melon de Bourgogne
Alcohol: 12%

Pleasant, light, zesty and crisp with crunchy apple
fruits and a lemony touch.
Perfect with seafood and lighter fish dishes.

Stockists: Almost nationwide – Tesco

XEROLITHIA PEZA 2003
Crete, Greece
€7.89

Grape: Vilana
Alcohol: 11.5%

Some very different but wonderful flavours—zingy, limy and dry, with a delicious honeyed flavour. Good with something light and tasty. Salads would be great. Why not try tzatziki?

Stockists: Dublin – Oddbins

ROUND AND FRUITY WHITE

Round and fruity white wines have richer flavours than the light and refreshing wines in the previous section. They feel heavier and fruitier in the mouth. Some have also been treated with oak, and have spicy flavours too. They can still be drunk on their own, but will also go very nicely with richer fish dishes as well as chicken and pork.

ADOBE CHARDONNAY 2004
Casablanca Valley, Chile
€9.95

Grape: Chardonnay
Alcohol: 14.1%

The rich alcohol is well hidden in a delicious fresh wine, full of racy green apples and grapefruits, finishing dry.
Fairly full-bodied, so it would go best with richer fish (monkfish, black sole), chicken and pork too.

Stockists: Dublin – O'Briens Wine Off-licences

BLUE WHITE CHENIN BLANC 2004
Coastal Region, South Africa
€9.99

Grape: Chenin Blanc
Alcohol: 13.5%

Pure, concentrated green fruits—fresh, medium-bodied wine with a great finish. Ignore the slightly naff blue bottle—this is a serious wine at a very good price.
Another all-purpose white—you could quite happily drink this on its own, but it would go equally well with fish or chicken.

Stockists: Almost nationwide – Superquinn. **Dublin** – Shiels' Londis, Malahide; SPAR, Milltown. **Kilkenny** – Centra, Kilkenny

BODEGAS LAVAQUE
TORRONTÉS 2004
Cafayate, Argentina
€9.99

Grape: Torrontés
Alcohol: 13.5%

An unusual but very enjoyable wine, with creamy smooth pineapple and elderflower fruits—layers of flavour that grow as you drink more.
This would be great with the bigger fish and chicken dishes. Try it with herby, spicy oriental foods.

Stockists: Cork – O'Donovan's, Cork. **Dublin** – Jus de Vine, Portmarnock; Kelly's Wine Vault, Artane; McHugh's, Kilbarrack & Artane; Red Island Wines, Skerries; Shiels' Londis, Malahide; The Lord Mayor's, Swords. **Louth** – Egan's, Drogheda

CHANSON MÂCON-VILLAGES 2004
Burgundy, France
€9.99

Grape: Chardonnay
Alcohol: 13%

Fantastic value with very appealing ripe, rounded apple fruits.
A fairly full-bodied wine that would go very nicely with chicken or pork, as well as the bolder fish dishes.

Stockists: Dublin – O'Briens Wine Off-licences

CONCHA Y TORO SUNRISE SAUVIGNON BLANC 2004
Central Valley, Chile
€8.99

Grape: Sauvignon Blanc
Alcohol: 13%

Medium-bodied, fresh grapefruit and pears, with a nice, crisp, dry finish.
This would make a great refreshing aperitif, or you could try it with herby or spicy chicken and fish.

Stockists: Almost nationwide – Centra; Londis; Superquinn. **Cork** – Bradley's; Next Door, Kinsale Rd; O'Sullivan's, Ballincollig; SPAR, Skibbereen. **Dublin** – Carvill's, Camden St; Cellars Wine Warehouse, Naas Rd; Coolers, Swords; Corks, Terenure; *(continued on next page)*

Delaney's, Aungier St; Deveney's, South Circular Rd & Dundrum;
Donnybrook Fair; Higgins, Clonskeagh; Lilac Wines, Fairview;
McHugh's, Kilbarrack & Artane; No. One Vintage, Goatstown;
O'Briens Wine Off-licences; Rialto House; Savage's, Swords; The
Best Cellar, Coolock; The Drink Store, Manor St; The Strand Off-
licence, Fairview; The Village Cellar, Swords; Whelan's, Wexford
St. **Kildare** – O'Rourkes, Newbridge. **Limerick** – Player's, Limerick.
Meath – The Bunch of Grapes, Clonee; The Wine Bottle,
Dunshaughlin. **Roscommon** – Clarke's, Boyle. **Sligo** – Foley's,
Sligo. **Waterford** – Next Door, Waterford

D'ARENBERG
STUMP JUMP WHITE 2004
South Australia
€9.95

Grape: Riesling, Sauvignon Blanc, Marsanne
Alcohol: 13%

Another very attractive, fragrant, rounded, richly fruity wine—the sort that made Oz famous, and rightly so—a real crowd pleaser.
A perfect all-rounder—for parties or before dinner.

Stockists: Cavan – Blessing's, Cavan. **Donegal** – Dicey Reilly's, Ballyshannon. **Dublin** – Boomers, Clondalkin; Bunch of Grapes, Donabate; Carvill's, Camden St; Cheers at The Laurels, Perrystown; Cheers at The Silver Granite, Palmerstown; Gibney's, Malahide; Lilac Wines, Fairview; Red Island Wines, Skerries; SuperValu, Killester; The Grape Escape, Lucan; Unwined, Swords. **Galway** – Morton's, Salthill, Galway. **Kerry** – Galvin's, Listowel. **Kilkenny** – The Wine Centre, Kilkenny. **Louth** – Egan's, Drogheda. **Limerick** – Mac's, Limerick. **Louth** – Peter Matthews, Drogheda. **Mayo** – Fahy's, Ballina. **Meath** – The Stone House, Navan. **Westmeath** – Artisans, Athlone; The Old Stand, Mullingar. **Wicklow** – Lakes, Blessington; Murtagh's, Enniskerry; Wicklow Wine Co., Wicklow

FINCA LA LINDA VIOGNIER 2004
Mendoza, Argentina
€9.99

Grape: Viognier
Alcohol: 13.5%

A big, rich wine, full of luscious tropical fruits—
pears, apricots—with a lovely creamy texture.
Viognier goes very well with grilled or roast chicken,
along with barbecued fish and most spicy oriental
foods.

Stockists: Almost nationwide – Next Door. **Dublin** – Claudio's,
Drury St; Donnybrook Fair; Gibney's, Malahide; Liston's, Camden
St; On the Grapevine, Dalkey & Booterstown. **Galway** – Morton's,
Salthill, Galway. **Wicklow** – Halpin's Fine Wines, Wicklow & Gorey

FINCA LAS MORAS VIOGNIER 2004
San Juan, Argentina
€7.99

Grape: Viognier
Alcohol: 13.5%

Lovely pure ripe peaches and cream, finishing with a pleasant, slightly bitter fruit-stone note.
A full-bodied white that calls for something substantial—barbecues, grilled chicken or maybe paella.

Stockists: Dublin – Cellars Wine Warehouse, Naas Rd; Higgins, Clonskeagh; Jus de Vine, Portmarnock; Londis, Manor St; On the Grapevine, Dalkey & Booterstown; Red Island Wines, Skerries; Shiels' Londis, Malahide; SPAR, Kimmage; The Kinsealy Inn; The Old Orchard, Rathfarnham; The Submarine Bar, Crumlin. **Galway** – The Vineyard, Galway. **Kildare** – Applegreen, Newbridge. The Mill Wine Cellar, Maynooth. **Kilkenny** – The Wine Centre, Kilkenny. **Louth** – Egan's, Drogheda. **Laois** – Portlaoise Wine Vault. **Meath** – Coolers, Clonee; O'Dwyer's, Navan. **Wicklow** – Cheers at The Wicklow Arms, Delgany

GOLD LABEL RESERVE CHARDONNAY VIN DE PAYS DE L'HÉRAULT, 2004
South of France
€8.99

Grape: Chardonnay
Alcohol: 12.5%

A big, rich, full-flavoured wine stuffed with ripe apple fruits and spicy oak flavours.
This would work very nicely with grilled or barbecued chicken and fish.

Stockists: Almost nationwide – Marks & Spencer

JACOB'S CREEK
RIESLING 2004
South East Australia
€9.95

Grape: Riesling
Alcohol: 11.5%

Medium-bodied, nicely rounded apple fruits, and a very refreshing lemon touch.
I would be tempted to try this with Asian dishes, mixed salads, or pâtés and rillettes, but, to be honest, this would be great as a party wine, or with all sorts of fish, chicken or pork dishes.

Stockists: Almost nationwide – Centra; Dunnes Stores; Gala; Mace; SPAR; SuperValu; Superquinn; Tesco. **Cork** – Blarney Off-licence; Hollyhill Liquor Store, Cork. **Clare** – Jayne's, Ennis. **Donegal** – Gallagher's, Donegal. **Dublin** – McHugh's, Kilbarrack & Artane; Molloy's Liquor Stores; Nolan's, Clontarf; O'Briens Wine Off-licences; Quinn's, Drumcondra; Savage's, Swords; The Strand Off-licence, Fairview. **Galway** – Harvest, Galway & Oranmore; Joyce's, Galway & Headford. **Kerry** – Castle Street Off-licence, Tralee; The Coin Off-licence, Tralee. **Kildare** – The Mill Wine Cellar, Maynooth. **Limerick** – Champers, Limerick; Fine Wines, Limerick. **Leitrim** – Greenan, Mohill.
(continued on next page)

Longford – Railway Bar, Longford. **Laois** – The Wine Vault, Portlaoise. **Meath** – Carroll's, Kells. **Mayo** – Corner Store, Ballina; Sweeney Oil, Westport. **Sligo** – Foley's, Sligo. **Tipperary** – O'Connor's, Nenagh. **Wexford** – Pettit's Supermarkets; Reid's, Enniscorthy. **Wicklow** – Ta Ses, Wicklow

LINDEMANS BIN 65 CHARDONNAY 2004
South East Australia
€9.99

Grape: Chardonnay
Alcohol: 13.5%

Classic modern Aussie Chardonnay—medium-bodied, rounded fresh apple fruits, with a light smoky, buttery edge.
A good choice for most white meat dishes, roast chicken in particular.

Stockists: Almost nationwide – Centra; Dunnes Stores; Eurospar; SuperValu; Superquinn; Tesco. **Cork** – Lynch's, Glanmire. **Dublin** – Martha's Vineyard, Rathfarnham; McHugh's, Kilbarrack & Artane; Redmond's, Ranelagh; Savage's, Swords. **Galway** – Joyce's, Galway & Headford. **Limerick** – Fine Wines, Limerick. **Sligo** – Currids. **Waterford** – Ardkeen Stores, Waterford

MICHEL TORINO TORRONTÉS 2004
Cafayate, Argentina
€9.99

Grape: Torrontés
Alcohol: 13.5%

Full-bodied, but intensely fruity wine, with textured layers of pineapples and peaches, finishing quite dry. This should go very nicely with oriental fish, chicken and pork dishes.

Stockists: Almost nationwide – Dunnes Stores. **Cork** – The Naked Grape, McCurtain St, Cork. **Dublin** – Cheers at Martin's Pub, Finglas; Cheers at The Laurels, Perrystown; Gibney's, Malahide; Martin's, Marino; No. One Vintage, Goatstown; The Best Cellar, Coolock; The Drink Store, Manor St; Galway – Harvest, Galway & Oranmore. **Kildare** – Next Door, Kavanagh's, Naas. **Limerick** – Coasters, Limerick; Cooper's Wine Superstore, Limerick. **Wicklow** – Murtagh's, Enniskerry. **Wexford** – The Diplomat, Dungarvan

MITCHELTON BLACKWOOD PARK ESTATE RIESLING 2004

Central Victoria, Australia

€9.99

Grape: Riesling
Alcohol: 13.5%

Mouth-watering, fresh wine with tingling lime and crisp green fruits; medium-bodied, with a dry finish. A good choice for most fish dishes, light lunches, or as a glass before dinner.

Stockists: Almost nationwide – Dunnes Stores

MITCHELTON THOMAS MITCHELL MARSANNE 2004

South Australia

€8.99

Grape: Marsanne
Alcohol: 13.5%

Rich, textured pears and mango overlaid with a touch of honey, all kept in balance by some mouth-watering acidity.
This would go down a treat with richer seafood dishes—prawns, scallops or crab.

Stockists: Almost nationwide – Dunnes Stores.
Dublin – Oddbins

PASCUAL TOSO SAUVIGNON 2004
Mendoza, Argentina
€9.99

Grape: Sauvignon Blanc
Alcohol: 14%

An unusual but very tasty Sauvignon, rich and powerful, with a heart-warming 14% alcohol and broad aromatic fruits.

A wine this powerful needs substantial food—goats' cheese goes well with Sauvignon, or maybe an oily fish such as sardines or tuna.

Stockists: Cork – O'Donovan's, Cork. Dublin – Jus de Vine, Portmarnock; Redmond's, Ranelagh; The Grape Escape, Lucan; The Vintry, Rathgar. **Galway** – The Vineyard, Galway; The Wine Cluster, Moycullen. **Kildare** – The Mill Wine Cellar, Maynooth. **Mayo** – Gaffney's, Ballina & Castlebar. **Sligo** – Currids. **Westmeath** – Cana Off-licence, Mullingar

SAINT HALLETT
POACHER'S BLEND 2003
Barossa Valley, Australia
€9.49

Grape: Semillon, Riesling, Colombard, Sauvignon Blanc
Alcohol: 12.5%

I love this style—very tasty, plump, quite rounded wine full of soft-bodied ripe green fruits.
Very nice on its own, or with salads and cold dishes.

Stockists: Dublin – Oddbins

SIMONSIG CHENIN BLANC 2004
Stellenbosch, South Africa
€7.99

Grape: Chenin Blanc
Alcohol: 14%

A full-bodied but fresh wine with textured palate-filling ripe pears and melons.
Ideal with chicken, pork and fish, particularly Thai or oriental dishes.

Stockists: Dublin – Eurospar, Lucan; Martha's Vineyard, Rathfarnham; Molloy's Liquor Stores; Nolan's, Clontarf; Rowan's, Rathfarnham; Sandyford House; SuperValu, Killester; SuperValu, Raheny; The Vintry, Rathgar. **Galway** – The Vineyard, Galway; **Louth** – Callan's, Dundalk; **Mayo** – Gaffney's, Ballina & Castlebar; **Meath** – O'Dwyer's, Navan; **Wicklow** – Fullam's, Rathangan; **Waterford** – Waterford World of Wine

TESCO'S FINEST
SOUTH AFRICAN CHENIN BLANC
2004
Stellenbosch, South Africa
€8.99

Grape: Chenin Blanc
Alcohol: 13%

Full-bodied, rich, with melons, pears and even peaches, kept fresh by some tangy grapefruit acidity. This would be great with oriental or fusion chicken and fish dishes, although I regularly drink it on its own.

Stockists: Almost nationwide – Tesco

THE ORACLE CHARDONNAY 2004
Western Cape, South Africa
€8.49

Grape: Chardonnay
Alcohol: 13.5%

Fresh, but quite full-bodied with stylish textured pears, melons and apples.
A good all-purpose white that will sit happily alongside most fish, white meats, creamy pasta, or all on its own.

Stockists: Almost nationwide – Centra; Dunnes Stores; SuperValu; Superquinn; Tesco

TRIVENTO VIOGNIER 2003
Mendoza, Argentina
€8.99

Grape: Viognier
Alcohol: 13%

Lovely fresh peaches and apples—soft, rounded and smooth, ending on a dry note.
This would make a great rich aperitif wine. It would also go very nicely with spicy Indian foods, and more full-flavoured white-fish dishes—monkfish, cod or grilled fish.

Stockists: Cork – Next Door, Kinsale Rd; O'Donovan's, Cork; SPAR, Skibbereen. **Dublin** – Cabot & Co., IFSC; Cellars Wine Warehouse, Naas Rd; Cheers at The Arc, Liffey Valley Shopping Centre; Coolers, Swords; *(continued on next page)*

Deveney's, South Circular Rd & Dundrum; Firhouse Inn; Gibney's, Malahide; McCabe's, Blackrock & Foxrock; Morton's, Ranelagh; O'Briens Wine Off-licences; On the Grapevine, Dalkey & Booterstown; Redmond's, Ranelagh; Rowan's, Rathfarnham; Savage's, Swords; The Coach House, Ballinteer; The Drink Store, Manor St; The Strand Off-licence, Fairview; The Submarine Bar, Crumlin; **Kildare** – Clane Service Station. **Kilkenny** – Eurospar, Dunmore; Next Door, Thomastown; The Wine Centre, Kilkenny. **Limerick** – CD Stores, Limerick; Next Door, Raheen; The Old Stand, Limerick. **Louth** – Egan's, Drogheda. **Meath** – Next Door, Navan; The Bunch of Grapes, Clonee; The Wine Bottle, Dunshaughlin. **Westmeath** – Bambricks, Mullingar. **Wicklow** – Cheers at The Wicklow Arms, Delgany. **Wexford** – Culletons, Kilrane; Greenacres, Wexford. **Waterford** – Next Door, Waterford

YALI CHARDONNAY 2004
Rapel Valley, Chile
€9.99

Grape: Chardonnay
Alcohol: 13.5%

Very stylish rounded ripe apple fruits, finishing fresh and dry.
Unoaked Chardonnay such as this is a great all-purpose wine either by itself or with a huge range of foods.

Stockists: Almost nationwide – Carry-Out Stores

ROSÉ

Rosés are fast becoming the fashionable drink in Ireland. They vary in style, from wonderfully light and fruity wines, perfect for drinking by themselves or with light lunches; to the more full-bodied wines, richer in alcohol and fruit, and better drunk alongside food.

CHIVITE GRAN FEUDO NAVARRA ROSÉ 2004
North Spain
€8.99

Grape: Garnacha
Alcohol: 12.5%

Light, crisp and dry, with very stylish, elegant, fresh, ripe strawberry fruits.
Perfect on a summer's day, but you could certainly drink it with richer fish such as tuna and salmon, or chicken throughout the year.

Stockists: Almost nationwide – Centra; Gala; Londis; Next Door; SPAR; SuperValu; Superquinn. **Dublin** – Bourke's Fine Wines, Cabinteely; Carvill's, Camden St; Eurospar, Killiney; Frank Kelly's, Chapelizod; Goggin's, Monkstown; Kelly's, Phibsboro; *(continued on next page)*

Martha's Vineyard, Rathfarnham; Martin's, Marino; McCabe's, Blackrock & Foxrock; McHugh's, Kilbarrack & Artane; Molloy's Liquor Stores; Morton's, Ranelagh; O'Brien's Wine Off-licences; On the Grapevine, Dalkey & Booterstown; Quinn's, Drumcondra; Robert Mooney, Ballsbridge; Teggart's, Rathgar; The Comet, Santry; The Grape Escape, Lucan; Unwined, Swords. **Kerry** – The Coin Off-licence, Tralee. **Kildare** – The Mill Wine Cellar, Maynooth. **Limerick** – Doneraile Stores, Limerick. **Louth** – Egan's, Drogheda. **Waterford** – Ardkeen Stores, Waterford. **Wicklow** – Caprani's, Ashford. **Wexford** – Pettit's Supermarkets

DOMAINE DE BEGUDE
PINOT ROSÉ
VIN DE PAYS DE L'AUDE 2004
South of France
€6.99

Grape: Pinot Noir
Alcohol: 12.5%

Light floral and cherry aromas, and delicious fresh, light red summer fruits, finishing crisp and dry. Ideal for drinking outside on a warm, sunny summer's day.

Stockists: Dublin – Molloy's Liquor Stores

FLAGSTONE SEMAPHORE ROSÉ 2004
Western Cape, South Africa
€7.99

Grape: Pinotage, Cabernet Franc, Sauvignon Blanc
Alcohol: 13.5%

A very crisp dry rosé, with lively mineral notes alongside some delicious ripe strawberry fruits. A classic summer wine, but this would also partner bigger fish dishes, as well as salad-type lunches.

Stockists: Dublin – Oddbins

GEOFF MERRILL
GRENACHE ROSÉ 2004
South Australia
€8.99

Grape: Grenache
Alcohol: 14%

Rosé with attitude—masses of big, juicy, ripe strawberry fruits, and plenty of alcohol to back it up. Try it while sitting around the barbecue waiting for the meat to cook, or with grilled fish or chicken dishes.

Stockists: Almost nationwide – Superquinn. **Dublin** – Bourke's Fine Wines, Cabinteely; Coolers, Swords; Higgins, Clonskeagh; Jus de Vine, Portmarnock; Martin's, Marino; The Goose, Drumcondra; **Kildare** – Applegreen, Newbridge. **Louth** – McPhail's, Drogheda. **Wexford** – The Sky and the Ground, Wexford

LIGHT AND ELEGANT RED

Light and elegant red wines have more subtle flavours and lighter fruit than the richer wines in the following two sections. They tend to be lower in alcohol, have fewer tannins, and feel less heavy in the mouth. Most can be drunk on their own, or with lighter meat, cheese and vegetarian dishes.

BROWN BROTHERS
TARRANGO 2004
Victoria, Australia
€9.99

Grape: Tarrango
Alcohol: 12.5%

Ripe, rounded dark fruits and cherries, with barely a whisper of tannin. In the summer you could chill it lightly. Tarrango is a grape variety developed for the hot, dry climate of Victoria.
Drink this on its own or with salads, cold meats or pies.

Stockists: Almost nationwide – Centra; Londis; Next Door; SPAR; SuperValu; Tesco. **Cork** – O'Donovan's, Cork; **Dublin** – McCabe's, Blackrock & Foxrock; McHugh's, Kilbarrack & Artane; Molloy's Liquor Stores

CHIVITE GRAN FEUDO NAVARRA CRIANZA 2002

North Spain

€9.99

Grape: Tempranillo, Garnacha, Cabernet Sauvignon
Alcohol: 12.5%

Light loganberry and blackberry fruits, with a dry, lightly tannic finish.
This would partner most meats, although lamb, either grilled or roast, would be traditional locally.

Stockists: Almost nationwide – Dunnes Stores; Next Door; SPAR; Superquinn. **Cork** – Carry-Out Stores, Hartes, Clonakilty. **Dublin** – Bennett's, Howth; Bourke's Fine Wines, Cabinteely; Carvill's, Camden St; Cellars Wine Warehouse, Naas Rd; Deveney's, South Circular Rd & Dundrum; Frank Kelly's, Chapelizod; Gibney's, Malahide; Goggin's, Monkstown; *(continued on next page)*

Goose Off-licence, Drumcondra; Hogan's, Rathfarnham; Jus de Vine, Portmarnock; Kelly's, Phibsboro; McCabe's, Blackrock & Foxrock; McHugh's, Kilbarrack & Artane; Molloy's Liquor Stores; Morton's, Ranelagh; Nolan's, Clontarf; O'Neills, South Circular Rd; On the Grapevine, Dalkey & Booterstown; Robert Mooney, Ballsbridge; Shiels' Londis, Malahide; Sweeney's, Glasnevin; The Lord Mayor's, Swords; The Strand Off-licence, Fairview; The Vintry, Rathgar; Unwined, Swords. **Galway** – The Vineyard, Galway. **Kildare** – O'Rourke's, Newbridge; The Mill Wine Cellar, Maynooth. **Kilkenny** – The Wine Centre, Kilkenny. **Longford** – Donlon's, Longford. **Louth** – Egan's, Drogheda. **Laois** – Portlaoise Wine Vault. **Limerick** – The Vineyard, Limerick. **Meath** – The Wine Well, Dunboyne. **Tipperary** – Lonergan's, Clonmel; Walsh, Templemore. **Wicklow** – Caprani's, Ashford. **Wexford** – Pettit's Supermarkets

CONO SUR PINOT NOIR 2003
Colchagua, Chile
€7.99

Grape: Pinot Noir
Alcohol: 13.5%

Probably the best-value Pinot Noir in the country—
lovely rounded, easy, juicy cherry fruits and a soft
finish.
Great on its own, also possibly with tuna or salmon,
certainly with poultry and game.

Stockists: Almost nationwide – Centra; Eurospar; Londis;
Mace. **Cork** – O'Donovan's, Cork. **Dublin** – Cellars Wine
Warehouse, Naas Rd; Gerry's, Skerries; Jus de Vine, Portmarnock;
Martha's Vineyard, Rathfarnham; Nolan's, Clontarf; Savage's,
Swords. **Galway** – Joyce's, Galway & Headford. **Meath** – The
Wine Well, Dunboyne. **Waterford** – Ardkeen Stores, Waterford

MISSION SAINT VINCENT BORDEAUX 2001
Bordeaux, France
€7.99

Grape: Merlot, Cabernet Sauvignon
Alcohol: 12%

A lovely, gentle, light wine with ripe blackcurrant fruits and an elegant dry finish.
You could drink it by itself, but it would go very nicely with the Sunday lunch, either lamb or beef, or plainly grilled white and red meats.

Stockists: Dublin – Molloy's Liquor Stores

OTTO BESTUÉ SOMONTANO 2003
North Spain
€9.99

Grape: Cabernet Sauvignon, Tempranillo
Alcohol: 13.5%

Light, elegant summer fruits and blackcurrants with a smoky touch, just enough acidity to keep real interest, and a stylish, smooth finish.
Nothing too big or powerful with this—I would try it on its own, or with lighter chicken, lamb and pork dishes.

Stockists: Almost nationwide – Dunnes Stores

RENZO MASI CHIANTI 2003
Tuscany, Italy
€9.99

Grape: Sangiovese, Canaiolo
Alcohol: 12.5%

A lovely, light, smooth Chianti with mild, elegant
cherry fruits.
Have it with a wide variety of Italian foods—
antipasti, pork or creamy pasta dishes.

Stockists: Wexford – Pettit's Supermarkets

SIERRA CANTABRIA RIOJA 2003
North Spain
€9.99

Grape: Tempranillo
Alcohol: 13.5%

Delightful, soft, light, elegant strawberry fruits with vanilla and spice. Smooth, silky and hard to resist. Lamb would be the classic match, but this is light and smooth enough to drink on its own, or with lighter foods.

Stockists: Dublin – O'Briens Wine Off-licences

RICH AND FRUITY RED

Rich and fruity reds are often great all-purpose wines, smooth, rounded and fruity enough to be drunk on their own, but with sufficient body to match a wide variety of foods.

AFRICAN ROCK PINOTAGE 2003
Western Cape, South Africa
€6.49

Grape: Pinotage
Alcohol: 13%

Very ripe, almost sweet, very smooth raspberry and
cherry fruits—lovely, soft, easy drinking.
A real all-purpose wine, perfect on its own, with white
meats, or lighter red-meat dishes and cheese.

Stockists: Almost nationwide – Aldi

ANTINORI SANTA CRISTINA IGT TOSCANA 2003

Tuscany, Italy

€9.99

Grape: Sangiovese, Merlot
Alcohol: 12.5%

Medium-bodied with tangy ripe black cherries and some light tannins on the finish.
Perfect with many Italian foods—especially those with tomato sauces. A good option for stuffed aubergines and peppers, too.

Stockists: Almost nationwide – Eurospar; Londis; SuperValu; Superquinn; Tesco. **Dublin** – Cellars Wine Warehouse, Naas Rd; Gourmet Shop, Rathgar; Jus de Vine, Portmarnock; Martha's Vineyard, Rathfarnham; McCabe's, Blackrock & Foxrock; Molloy's Liquor Stores; Nolan's, Clontarf; O'Briens Wine Off-licences; Redmond's, Ranelagh. **Limerick** – Ivan's, Caherdavin

CASILLERO DEL DIABLO
MERLOT 2004
Rapel Valley, Chile
€9.99

Grape: Merlot
Alcohol: 13.5%

Classic Chilean Merlot—plenty of ripe plums and blackcurrants with light drying tannins on the finish. As with most Merlots, a great all-purpose wine, suited to most meat and vegetable dishes, and good on its own.

Stockists: Almost nationwide – Centra; Dunnes Stores; Londis; Next Door; SuperValu; Tesco. **Cork** – Bradley's; O'Donovan's, Cork. **Dublin** – Cellars Wine Warehouse, Naas Rd; Higgins, Clonskeagh; Lilac Wines, Fairview; McCabe's, Blackrock & Foxrock; Molloy's Liquor Stores; No. One Vintage, Goatstown; *(continued on next page)*

Nolan's, Clontarf; O'Briens Wine Off-licences; Oddbins; Raheny
Wine Cellar; The Drink Store, Manor St; The Orchard, Applewood;
Galway – Harvest, Galway & Oranmore; Joyce's, Galway &
Headford; The Vineyard, Galway. **Kerry** – O'Driscoll's,
Caherciveen; The Castle Off-licence, Tralee. **Limerick** –
Champers, Limerick. **Louth** – McManus, Dundalk. **Mayo** –
Gaffney's, Ballina & Castlebar. **Wicklow** – Cheers at The Wicklow
Arms, Delgany. **Wexford** – Pettit's Supermarkets

CASTILLO PERELADA COSTA BRAVA CRIANZA 2001

Catalonia, Spain

€9.99

Grape: Garnacha, Cariñena, Tempranillo
Alcohol: 13.5%

Wonderful ripe cassis fruits with a creamy, smooth texture and a lightly dry finish.
This would partner a wide variety of white- or red-meat dishes. Try it with roast lamb—a rack would do very nicely.

Stockists: Dublin – Bin No. 9, Goatstown; Boomers, Clondalkin; Martin's, Marino; No. One Vintage, Goatstown; SPAR, Ballycullen The Vintry, Rathgar; Unwined, Swords. **Louth** – Callan's, Dundalk

CHÂTEAU LA GRAVE CUVÉE EXPRESSION MINERVOIS 2002
South of France
€9.99

Grape: Syrah, Grenache, Mourvèdre
Alcohol: 13%

Warm, ripe cherry fruits with plenty of oomph, and a dry finish.
Great with medium-bodied foods—pork and chicken casseroles, milder cheeses and pasta dishes or vegetable couscous.

Stockists: Almost nationwide – Next Door. **Donegal** – McGrory's, Culdaff. **Dublin** – Morton's, Ranelagh; Redmond's, Ranelagh; Searson's, Monkstown. **Limerick** – Mac's, Limerick. **Sligo** – Patrick Stewart Wines, Sligo. **Wexford** – Pettit's Supermarkets

CONO SUR MERLOT 2004
Central Valley, Chile
€7.99

Grape: Merlot
Alcohol: 14%

Packed with deliciously ripe, smooth plum fruits, with a lightly peppery finish.
A very versatile wine that suits most dishes, including pizza and pasta.

Stockists: Almost nationwide – Dunnes Stores; Eurospar; SuperValu; Tesco. **Cork** – O'Donovan's, Cork. **Dublin** – Cellars Wine Warehouse, Naas Rd; Nolan's, Clontarf; Redmond's, Ranelagh; Savage's, Swords. **Galway** – Harvest, Galway & Oranmore; Joyce's, Galway & Headford. **Limerick** – CD Stores, Limerick; Mac's, Limerick. **Meath** – The Wine Well, Dunboyne **Waterford** – Ardkeen Stores, Waterford

DOMAINE CAZAL-VIEL SAINT CHINIAN VIEILLES VIGNES 2003
South of France
€8.99

Grape: Syrah, with a small amount of Mourvèdre, Carignan & Cinsault
Alcohol: 13.5%

An excellent, big, rich, hearty wine, brimming with delicious rustic fruits, with some lovely ripe tannins on the finish. One of my favourite wines. 'Vieilles Vignes' on a label means that the vines used to make the wine are at least 25 years old.
I would happily drink this with virtually any meat or cheese dish, including pasta.

Stockists: Almost nationwide – Tesco

ERRÁZURIZ
CABERNET SAUVIGNON 2003
Aconcagua Valley, Chile
€9.99

Grape: Cabernet Sauvignon
Alcohol: 14%

Classic Chilean Cabernet—ripe blackcurrants and plums, offset by light tannins on a dry finish.
The tannins would fade with food. It would go very nicely with most white or red meats.

Stockists: Almost nationwide – Dunnes Stores; SuperValu; Superquinn; Tesco. **Cork** – Bradley's. **Clare** – Jayne's, Ennis. **Cork** – Lynch's, Glanmire; Scally's, Cork. **Dublin** – KCR Stores, Terenure; Lymay's, Goatstown; Quinn's, Drumcondra; Savage's, Swords; Teggart's, Rathgar; The Drink Store, Manor St. **Galway** – Joyce's, Galway & Headford. **Limerick** – Champers, Limerick; The Vineyard, Limerick. **Meath** – Wine Well, Dunboyne

ERRÁZURIZ MERLOT 2004
Curicó Valley, Chile
€9.99

Grape: Merlot
Alcohol: 14%

A consistent favourite over the years. Some lovely fresh red fruits, with a nice spicy/coffee edge, and light, ripe tannins on a dryish finish.
This is the sort of wine that goes with pretty much everything, from pizza to pasta to most meat dishes.

Stockists: Almost nationwide – Dunnes Stores; SuperValu; Superquinn; Tesco. **Cork** – Bradley's; Lynch's, Glanmire; Scally's, Cork. **Clare** – Jayne's, Ennis. **Dublin** – KCR Stores, Terenure; Lymay's, Goatstown; Quinn's, Drumcondra; Savage's, Swords; Teggart's, Rathgar; The Drink Store, Manor St. **Galway** – Joyce's, Galway & Headford. **Limerick** – Champers, Limerick; The Vineyard, Limerick. **Meath** – Wine Well, Dunboyne

HUTTON RIDGE MERLOT 2003
Coastal Region, South Africa
€8.99

Grape: Merlot
Alcohol: 14.5%

Abundant soft, ripe, plummy fruits, with a
surprisingly good smooth follow-through.
The perfect everyday, all-purpose wine, to drink by
itself or with a wide variety of foods, including
vegetable dishes.

Stockists: Cork – The Nook, Youghal. **Dublin** – Centra, Coolock;
The Grapevine, Glasnevin. **Limerick** – Centra, Adare; Costcutter,
Foynes. **Wicklow** – Centra, Fossa. **Waterford** – Centra, Tallow

JACOB'S CREEK GRENACHE/SHIRAZ 2004
South East Australia
€7.95

Grape: Grenache, Shiraz
Alcohol: 14%

Some lovely soft, sweet strawberry fruits are given a bit of backbone by the plummy Shiraz flavours and light tannins.
This would be a good match for rich pastas, vegetarian bakes, and lighter meat dishes.

Stockists: Almost nationwide – Centra; Dunnes Stores; Gala; Mace; SuperValu; Superquinn; Tesco. **Cork** – Blarney Off-licence; Hollyhill Liquor Store, Cork. **Clare** – Jayne's, Ennis. **Donegal** – Gallagher's, Donegal. **Dublin** – McHugh's, Kilbarrack & Artane; Molloy's Liquor Stores; Nolan's, Clontarf; O'Briens Wine Off-licences; Quinn's, Drumcondra; Savage's, Swords; The Strand Off-licence, Fairview. **Galway** – Harvest, Galway & Oranmore; Joyce's, Galway & Headford. **Kerry** – Castle Street Off-licence, Tralee; The Coin Off-licence, Tralee. **Kildare** – The Mill Wine Cellar, Maynooth. **Limerick** – Champers, Limerick; Fine Wines, Limerick.
(continued on next page)

Leitrim – Greenan, Mohill. **Longford** – Railway Bar, Longford. **Laois** – The Wine Vault, Portlaoise. **Meath** – Carroll's, Kells. **Mayo** – Corner Store, Ballina; Sweeney Oil, Westport. **Sligo** – Foley's, Sligo. **Tipperary** – O'Connor's, Nenagh. **Wexford** – Pettit's Supermarkets; Reid's, Enniscorthy. **Wicklow** – Ta Ses, Wicklow

LA FORGE ESTATE MERLOT VIN DE PAYS D'OC 2003
South of France
€9.99

Grape: Merlot
Alcohol: 13%

Excellent pure, medium-bodied plum fruits, hints of chocolate and a peppery finish.
A good all-rounder that would suit most meats or cheese.

Stockists: Almost nationwide – SuperValu

LAURENT MIQUEL NORD SUD SYRAH VIN DE PAYS D'OC 2003
South of France
€9.99

Grape: Syrah
Alcohol: 13%

Wonderful pure, ripe dark fruits; medium-bodied, supple and smooth, with a lovely spicy finish.
A good all-rounder for white or red meats, but you could drink it on its own without a problem.

Stockists: Almost nationwide – Dunnes Stores

LINDEMANS BIN 50 SHIRAZ 2003
South East Australia
€9.99

Grape: Shiraz
Alcohol: 13.5%

Very yummy medium-bodied ripe plum fruits—
lively, fruity and smooth.
A good all-purpose wine—fine on its own, but it
would suit most meats and cheeses.

Stockists: Almost nationwide – Centra; Eurospar; Next Door;
SuperValu; Superquinn; Tesco. **Cork** – O'Donovan's, Cork.
Dublin – Carvill's, Camden St; Martha's Vineyard, Rathfarnham;
O'Briens Wine Off-licences; Quinn's, Drumcondra; Redmond's,
Ranelagh; Savage's, Swords. **Galway** – Joyce's, Galway &
Headford

MARQUÉS DE BALLESTAR
CARIÑENA CRIANZA 2000
North Spain
€8.99

Grape: Tempranillo, Garnacha
Alcohol: 13.5%

Lovely jammy ripe raspberry fruits, with a savoury,
tarry edge and a smooth finish.
Would go well with most lighter white- and red-meat
dishes. Try it with pork chops or roast pork.

Stockists: Dublin – Baily Wines, Howth; Burke & Burke,
Drumcondra; Cellars Wine Warehouse, Naas Rd;
Deveney's, South Circular Rd & Dundrum; Gibney's, Malahide;
Nolan's, Clontarf; O'Neill's, South Circular Rd; The Vintry, Rathgar

PLUME BLEUE VIN DE PAYS D'OC 2004

South of France

€8.99

Grape: Grenache, Syrah
Alcohol: 13%

One of the best-value warming reds around. Very tasty, ripe rounded fruit, with a lovely spicy kick. It has very light tannins so you could drink it by itself, although lamb or pork would be ideal.

Stockists: Cork – The Kitchen Project, Clonakilty. **Dublin** – Bin No. 9, Goatstown; Cabot & Co., IFSC; Cellars Wine Warehouse, Naas Rd; Donnybrook Fair; Martha's Vineyard, Rathfarnham; McCabe's, Blackrock & Foxrock; On the Grapevine, Dalkey & Booterstown; Red Island Wines, Skerries; Redmond's, Ranelagh; The Grape Escape, Lucan. **Galway** – The Vineyard, Galway. **Kildare** – The Mill Wine Cellar, Maynooth. **Mayo** – Gaffney's, Ballina & Castlebar. **Wicklow** – Wicklow Wine Co., Wicklow

QUINTA DE CABRIZ DÃO 2003
North Portugal
€9.50

Grape: Alfrocheiro, Tinta Roriz, Touriga Nacional
Alcohol: 13%

Very tasty, medium-bodied, chunky cherry fruits,
with some lightly refreshing acidity.
Good with lighter meat dishes—chicken or pork, but
you could also try it with tuna or grilled salmon.

Stockists: Dublin – The Grape Escape, Lucan. **Wicklow** –
Wicklow Wine Co., Wicklow

SAN PEDRO MERLOT 2004
Lontué Valley, Chile
€7.99

Grape: Merlot
Alcohol: 13%

Blackcurrants and plums in a soft, smooth, easy-drinking wine.
Another all-purpose red. You could drink it on its own, or with most white and red meats, as well as cheese dishes and pasta.

Stockists: Almost nationwide – Dunnes Stores

TERRE MEGERRE MERLOT
VIN DE PAYS D'OC 2003
South of France
€9.80

Grape: Merlot
Alcohol: 13%

A perennial favourite of mine from one of France's maverick artisan winemakers. Elegantly supple fruity Merlot, with a distinctly savoury dry finish.
A wine that really needs a bit of food, but a good all-rounder to drink with most meats or cheese.

Stockists: Westmeath – Wines Direct, Mullingar

TESCO'S FINEST RESERVE MERLOT 2004
Central Valley, Chile
€9.99

Grape: Merlot
Alcohol: 14%

Lovely, smooth, rich, pure, freshly crushed blackcurrants with a spicy edge, although be warned—this has a barely noticeable 14% alcohol! A food-friendly all-rounder that would happily go with most meat and cheese dishes.

Stockists: Almost nationwide – Tesco

TRIVENTO TRIBU MALBEC 2004
Mendoza, Argentina
€8.99

Grape: Malbec
Alcohol: 13.5%

Smooth, elegant red fruits, with a nice tangy element, and ripe tannins on the finish. Full-bodied, but juicy, easy drinking.
Fruity and smooth enough to drink by itself if you like full-bodied wines, or a fairly fail-safe match for most red meats, pork, game and cheese.

Stockists: Almost nationwide – SuperValu; Superquinn. **Cork** – Ardkeen Stores. **Cavan** – Donoghue's, Cavan; Next Door, Cavan. **Cork** – Next Door, Kinsale Rd; O'Donovan's, Cork. **Dublin** – Cheers at The Arc, Liffey Valley Shopping Centre;
(continued on next page)

Coolers, Swords; McCabe's, Blackrock & Foxrock; Morton's, Ranelagh; O'Briens Wine Off-licences; Savage's, Swords. **Galway** – Harvest, Galway & Oranmore; Joyce's, Galway & Headford; The Vineyard, Galway. **Kildare** – Clane Service Station. **Louth** – Egan's, Drogheda. **Limerick** – Next Door, Raheen; Old Stand, Limerick. **Tipperary** – Cooper's, Tipperary. **Westmeath** – Bambricks, Mullingar. **Wicklow** – Next Door, Arklow. **Waterford** – Next Door, Waterford. **Wexford** – Pettit's Supermarkets

UNDURRAGA MERLOT 2004
Colchagua, Chile
€8.99

Grape: Merlot
Alcohol: 13.5%

Clean, herbaceous edge to the slightly lean plum fruits. It would suit a lover of French wine; tangy, pleasant, better with food.
Merlot is great with a wide variety of foods, particularly medium-bodied dishes such as turkey, chicken and pork, as well as meat pies and pâtés.

Stockists: Almost nationwide – SPAR (selected stores); Superquinn. **Dublin** – Donnybrook Fair; Goggin's, Monkstown; *(continued on next page)*

JC's, Swords; Rowan's, Rathfarnham; The Comet, Santry; The Leopardstown Inn, Stillorgan; The Magic Carpet, Foxrock; The Vesey Arms, Lucan. **Louth** – Callan's, Dundalk. **Meath** – Killian's, Trim; O'Dwyer's, Navan

FULL-BODIED AND POWERFUL RED

Full-bodied and powerful reds
are the weight-lifters of the
wine styles—big, muscular
wines, full of fruit, with plenty
of alcohol and often substantial
tannins too. Because of their
sheer size, they are best suited
to heartier foods—red meats,
game, cheese, and pasta bakes.

ANDES PEAK SYRAH 2004
Rapel Valley, Chile
€9.95

Grape: Syrah
Alcohol: 14%

Full-bodied plum fruits, with a distinctive savoury black-olive note. A few dry tannins too. Chile is starting to make some great Syrah and this is a perfect example.
The powerful alcohol and dry tannins need something fairly robust—red meat or a strong cheese.

Stockists: Dublin – O'Briens Wine Off-licences

BODEGAS LAVAQUE SYRAH 2003
Cafayate, Argentina
€9.99

Grape: Syrah
Alcohol: 14%

This is a full-bodied but still nicely restrained wine, with very elegant dark fruits, hints of liquorice, and a delicious dry finish. Wonderful stuff—a perfect example of how Argentina offers real value at the moment.
Bring on the red meat—grilled, barbecued or roast!

Stockists: Cork – O'Donovan's, Cork. **Dublin** – Jus de Vine, Portmarnock; Kelly's Wine Vault, Artane; McHugh's, Kilbarrack & Artane; Red Island Wines, Skerries; Shiels' Londis, Malahide; The Lord Mayor's, Swords. **Louth** – Egan's, Drogheda

CARMEN
CABERNET SAUVIGNON 2003
Rapel Valley, Chile
€9.29

Grape: Cabernet Sauvignon
Alcohol: 14%

Very attractive fruit-laden wine with plenty of cassis and ripe red fruits, set off nicely by a dry finish. Ideal with red meat or game. A roast of beef or a steak would do nicely.

Stockists: Almost nationwide – Centra; Dunnes Stores; SuperValu; Superquinn; Tesco. **Dublin** – O'Briens Wine Off-licences. **Wexford** – Pettit's Supermarkets

CASTAÑO HÉCULA YECLA 2003
Murcia, Spain
€9.99

Grape: Monastrell
Alcohol: 14%

A big, burly wine full of figs, spice and dark red fruits, finishing with substantial savoury tannins.
Try it with something very robust—a juicy big steak, preferably barbecued, would be perfect, or a hearty winter casserole.

Stockists: Dublin – Deveney's, South Circular Rd & Dundrum; Donnybrook Fair; Gibney's, Malahide; Jus de Vine, Portmarnock; Martha's Vineyard, Rathfarnham; Morton's, Ranelagh; O'Neill's, South Circular Rd; On the Grapevine, Dalkey & Booterstown; Redmond's, Ranelagh; The Drink Store, Manor St; Unwined, Swords. **Kildare** – The Mill Wine Cellar, Maynooth. **Louth** – McPhail's, Drogheda. **Meath** – Killian's, Trim. **Wicklow** – The Wicklow Arms, Delgany

D'ARENBERG
STUMP JUMP RED 2004
South Australia
€9.95

Grape: Grenache, Syrah, Mourvèdre
Alcohol: 14%

Rich, rounded, ripe, soft strawberry fruits—a real glugger.
As with the white version, a great all-rounder that would go down dangerously well at a party.

Stockists: Cavan – Blessing's, Cavan. **Donegal** – Dicey Reilly's, Ballyshannon. **Dublin** – Boomers, Clondalkin; Bunch of Grapes, Donabate; Cabot & Co., IFSC; Carvill's, Camden St; Cheers at The Laurels, Perrystown. Gerry's, Skerries; Lilac Wines, Fairview; Martin's, Marino; McHugh's, Kilbarrack & Artane; Red Island Wines, Skerries; SPAR, Rathcoole; SuperValu, Raheny; The Grape Escape, Lucan; The Vintry, Rathgar; Unwined, Swords. **Galway** – Burke Londis, Kinvara; Maguire, Galway; Morton's, Salthill, Galway. **Kerry** – Galvin's, Listowel. **Kilkenny** – The Wine Centre, Kilkenny. **Limerick** – Mac's, Limerick. **Louth** – Egan's, Drogheda; Peter Matthews, Drogheda. **Mayo** – Fahy's, Ballina; Mac Namara, Louisburg. **Meath** – The Stone House, Navan. **Westmeath** – Artisans, Athlone. **Wicklow** – Lakes, Blessington; Murtagh's, Enniskerry; Wicklow Wine Co., Wicklow

INYCON MERLOT
IGT SICILIA 2003
Sicily, Italy
€7.99

Grape: Merlot
Alcohol: 13.5%

Big, ripe and juicy, with some very succulent damsons and plums.
Save this for when you are eating something robust—casseroles in the winter, barbecues or grills in the summer.

Stockists: Almost nationwide – Dunnes Stores

LA VIEILLE FERME
CÔTES DU VENTOUX
ROUGE 2003
Rhône Valley, France
€8.99

Grape: Grenache, Syrah, Mourvèdre, Carignan, Cinsault
Alcohol: 13.5%

Some lovely forward, ripe, juicy strawberry fruits, but packing a real punch too.
This calls for steak, roast meats, or a hearty bean casserole. In summer, try it with barbecues.

Stockists: Almost nationwide – Carry-Out Stores

La Vieille Ferme

CÔTES DU VENTOUX

MANDORLA SYRAH
IGT SICILIA 2003
Sicily, Italy
€9.00

Grape: Syrah
Alcohol: 13.5%

Firm, concentrated savoury liquorice and plum
fruits, with a dry finish.
Something fairly big and meaty called for here—
hearty, garlicky lamb or beef dishes would do very
nicely.

Stockists: Almost nationwide – Marks & Spencer

MICHEL TORINO
CABERNET SAUVIGNON 2004
Cafayate, Argentina
€9.99

Grape: Cabernet Sauvignon
Alcohol: 13.5%

Delicious intense pure blackcurrant fruits, with plenty of body and a dry finish.
A good match for most red meats, pork and hard cheeses. It has the power and body to cope with substantial flavours.

Stockists: Cavan – Blessing's, Cavan. **Carlow** – Carpenter's, Carlow. **Cork** – J J O'Driscoll, Ballinlough, Cork; Naked Grape, McCurtain St, Cork. **Dublin** – Baily Wines, Howth; Cheers at The Laurels, Perrystown; Martin's, Marino; No. One Vintage, Goatstown; The Best Cellar, Coolock; The Grapevine, Glasnevin. **Galway** – Harvest, Galway & Oranmore. **Limerick** – Coasters, Limerick; Cooper's Wine Superstore, Limerick. **Meath** – The Bunch of Grapes, Clonee. **Wexford** – The Diplomat, Dungarvan

MOORE'S CREEK SHIRAZ 2003
South East Australia
€9.99

Grape: Shiraz
Alcohol: 14.5%

Australia in a glass—delicious smooth, ripe plums and cassis, lingering in the mouth, and packing a real punch.

Food would be fairly essential, preferably something on the hearty side. Think red meat. Vegetarians could opt for baked mushrooms.

Stockists: Cork – O'Donovan's, Cork; SuperValu, Kinsale; SuperValu, Skibbereen. **Donegal** – SuperValu, Dungloe. **Dublin** – Goggin's, Monkstown; SuperValu, Churchtown; SuperValu, Killiney. **Galway** – SuperValu, Oranmore. **Kerry** – Centra, Dingle. **Kilkenny** – SuperValu, Kilkenny. **Limerick** – Champers, Limerick. **Louth** – SuperValu, Ardee. **Longford** – SuperValu, Longford. **Meath** – SuperValu, Trim. **Waterford** – Ardkeen Stores, Waterford

NUGAN ESTATE SHIRAZ 2003
South East Australia
€9.99

Grape: Shiraz
Alcohol: 14%

Classy, pure plum fruits, plenty of body, but very nicely balanced, coming together to make a very pleasant, smooth wine.
A fairly substantial wine that needs similar food—grilled Mediterranean vegetables, or meat, preferably pork, beef or any game.

Stockists: Almost nationwide – SuperValu

OLD VINES GRENACHE
CÔTES DU ROUSSILLON 2004
South of France
€8.50

Grape: Grenache
Alcohol: 14.5%

Big, rich, sweet, ripe, jammy strawberry fruits in a heady, full-bodied but smooth wine.
A midweek special—the soft, smooth fruit would take virtually anything you can think of—it would be great with pizza or pasta.

Stockists: Almost nationwide – Marks & Spencer

PREECE SHIRAZ 2003
Victoria, Australia
€9.99

Grape: Shiraz
Alcohol: 13.5%

Big, rich and powerful with chewy plum fruits and
hints of coffee.
This calls for something seriously big—barbecued
beef, hearty casseroles, and full-bodied game.

Stockists: Almost nationwide – Dunnes Stores

PROMESSA NEGROAMARO
IGT SALENTO 2003
Apulia, Italy
€9.95

Grape: Negroamaro
Alcohol: 13.5%

Full-bodied but ripe, smooth dark cherries and
plums with very attractive spicy oak.
Drink something fairly gutsy with this—roasts, grills
or barbecued beef, lamb or game.

Stockists: Dublin – Martha's Vineyard, Rathfarnham; Red Island
Wines, Skerries; The Grape Escape, Lucan. **Galway** – The
Vineyard, Galway. **Meath** – The Drinkstore, Navan. **Wexford** –
Pettit's Supermarkets

QUARA MALBEC 2004
Cafayate, Argentina
€8.95

Grape: Malbec
Alcohol: 13.5%

Delicious fresh loganberries and plums in a full-bodied, smooth, classy wine. Terrific value.
Beef would be the traditional choice to go with this wine, but it is smooth enough for most meat dishes, as well as hard cheeses.

Stockists: Dublin – Molloy's Liquor Stores

SAINT HALLETT GAMEKEEPER'S RESERVE 2003
Barossa Valley, Australia
€9.49

Grape: Shiraz, Grenache, plus Mataro & Touriga Nacional
Alcohol: 14.5%

Lovely ripe raspberry fruits with hints of smoke and tobacco, and plenty of warming alcohol.
A dangerously gluggable wine, perfect for those cold winter nights, or with barbecues.

Stockists: Dublin – Oddbins

SAN PEDRO RESERVA MERLOT 2003
Lontué Valley, Chile
€9.49

Grape: Merlot
Alcohol: 14%

Lovely ripe, smooth, rich plum fruits with a minty touch, and some vanilla spice—full-bodied and very classy.
The richness and power call for something equally big—game or a casserole. Alternatively, match the sweetness of the fruit with a baked ham.

Stockists: Almost nationwide – Dunnes Stores

SIMONSIG PINOTAGE 2001
Stellenbosch, South Africa
€9.99

Grape: Pinotage
Alcohol: 14%

Delicious, rich, full-bodied silky plum and dark cherry fruits, with a smoky touch.
This needs something fairly substantial to match the bold flavours—grilled meats, game or roasts.

Stockists: Cork – O'Donovan's, Cork. **Dublin** – Deveney's, South Circular Rd & Dundrum; Dublin – Eurospar, Lucan; Nolan's, Clontarf; Redmond's, Ranelagh; The Goose, Drumcondra. **Limerick** – Fine Wines, Limerick. **Meath** – O'Dwyer's, Navan; The Bottleshop, Sallins

THE WOLFTRAP 2004
Western Cape, South Africa
€8.99

Grape: Cabernet Sauvignon, Syrah, Cinsault
Alcohol: 14.5%

A rich, dark satisfying wine with smoky cherry fruits and a touch of chocolate. Smooth, but with a dry finish.
A full-bodied red that calls for red meat, either roast or barbecued. Vegetarians should think of ratatouille or something equally full-flavoured.

Stockists: Almost nationwide – Superquinn

VISCONDE DE BORBA
VR ALENTEJO 2003
South Portugal
€9.95

Grape: Trincadeira, Periquita, Aragonez
Alcohol: 13%

Easy, full-bodied, with smooth ripe red fruits and a nice tannic kick at the end.
You'll need some meat here—lamb or beef would be best, although locally they do a very good roast of pork.

Stockists: Dublin – Anderson's, Glasnevin; Mitchell & Son, Kildare St & Glasthule; The Grape Escape, Lucan. **Roscommon** – Heran's, Boyle

SHERRY

Sherry is a fantastic, misunderstood drink. Let me assure you—sherry is one of the great treats of the world of wine, and better still, it is one of the best-value wines you can buy.

The first three sherries listed here should be served chilled straight from the fridge and, once opened, drunk within a week.

Try these sherries as an aperitif (they are great with olives, toasted almonds and other nuts, crisps and all of the other nibbles) or drink them with seafood.

The final sherry, an Oloroso, is more of an after-dinner drink.

BARBADILLO MANZANILLA
Jerez, Spain
€9.99

Grape: Palomino Fino
Alcohol: 15%

Barbadillo is one of the top sherry houses, and its Manzanilla is one of the very best. Vibrant, pungent, very crisp and bone dry, it has a salty tang as well. Manzanilla is a form of fino sherry, with the same delicious nutty flavours—it is just a bit lighter, and fresher.

Stockists: Dublin – Oddbins

MARKS & SPENCER
FINO SHERRY NV
Jerez, Spain
€7.00

Grape: Palomino Fino
Alcohol: 15%

Incredible value—light, crisp and fresh with lovely tangy, nutty flavours, lively acidity, and a dry finish. Crab and fino sherry is a match made in heaven.

Stockists: Almost nationwide – Marks & Spencer

TESCO'S FINEST
FINO SHERRY NV
€9.99
Jerez, Spain

Grape: Palomino Fino
Alcohol: 15%

A lovely almondy nuttiness, finishing very dry with a
real tanginess.

Stockists: Almost nationwide – Tesco

TESCO'S FINEST
DRY OLOROSO NV
Jerez, Spain
€9.99

Grape: Palomino Fino
Alcohol: 18%

This is entirely different to the three sherries above.
Deep in colour, and full of dark woody flavours, it
should be served at room temperature.
Rich and full-bodied with intense flavours of walnuts,
raisins, spice and caramel, finishing dry. This is best
served after dinner with a hunk of cheese and a few
nuts, preferably walnuts.

Stockists: Almost nationwide – Tesco

SPARKLING WINES

Government duties on wine in this country are amongst the highest in Europe. Duties on sparkling wine are twice as high. You will pay almost €5 in tax before the cost of the wine is taken into account. Hardly surprising then that I have only included two sparkling wines under €10 in this book.

To improve matters slightly, I also recommend two of my favourite bottles of bubbly under €15, both of which are real bargains.

JACOB'S CREEK BRUT CUVÉE SPARKLING NV
Australia
€12.95

Grape: Chardonnay-Pinot Noir
Alcohol: 12%

Before you accuse me of being a shareholder in Jacob's Creek, let me assure you that the sole reason they have three entries in this book (see also white wines and red wines) is that some of the wines offer remarkable value for money.

The sparkling wine has lovely fresh, frothy medium-bodied apple fruits, vibrant acidity, and a very decent finish.

Sparkling wine is the celebration wine; it is the perfect aperitif; it also goes very well with a number of foods–oysters being the great match, but most seafood and fish will do very nicely.

Stockists: Almost nationwide – including Dunnes Stores, Tesco, and Supervalu.

LA RIVA DEI FRATI PROSECCO DI VALDOBBIADENE NV

Veneto, Italy

€14.50

Grape: Prosecco
Alcohol: 11.5%

Prosecco is one of the great Italian sparklers. Lighter and fruitier than a Champagne, it may not have quite the same complexity, but it does slip down beautifully.

Delicious, clean and light, with stylish fresh ripe pears and apple fruits, this is another ideal celebration wine. It is also perfect on a warm summer's day.

Stockists: Dublin – Cabot & Co., IFSC; Donnybrook Fair; Jus de Vine, Portmarknock; Louis Albrouze, Leeson St.; No.1 Vintage, Goatstown; On The Grapevine, Dalkey & Booterstown; Listons, Camden St; Red Island Wines, Skerries; The Grape Escape, Lucan. **Kilkenny** – Le Caveau, Kilkenny. **Mayo** – Gaffneys, Ballina. **Waterford** – World Wide Wines, Waterford. **Westmeath** – Cana Wines, Mullingar. **Wexford** – Pettitt's Supermarkets. **Wicklow** – Wicklow Wine Co., Wicklow; Murtagh's, Enniskerry.

PHILLIPPE MICHEL CRÈMANT DE JURA BRUT NV
Eastern France
€9.99

Grape: Chardonnay
Alcohol: 12%

Amazingly drinkable wine, considering over half of the purchase price goes on duty. Made from the Chardonnay grape (as used in Champagne), this is clean and light with very appetising fresh, crisp apple fruits.
You could drink it by itself, or use it as a base for a Kir Royale, Buck's Fizz or other cocktails.

Stockists: Almost nationwide – Aldi

TESCO'S ASTI NV
Northern Italy
€8.95

Grape: Moscato
Alcohol: 7%

Wine snobs will recoil with horror, but every now and again, I have a yearning for a glass of Asti Spumante, that sweet, aromatic fizz from Italy.
Fresh and aromatic with delicious elderflower and grapey fruits, finishing on a sweet note. The perfect drink with dessert, it can match the sweetness of the food, it's light, so it refreshes rather than sends you to sleep—and it's fun!

Stockists: Almost nationwide – Tesco